Write for M   per

Jacqueline Fahey

Copyright © 2015 Jacqueline Fahey

All rights reserved, including the right to reproduce this book, or portions thereof in any form. No part of this text may be reproduced, transmitted, downloaded, decompiled, reverse engineered, or stored, in any form or introduced into any information storage and retrieval system, in any form or by any means, whether electronic or mechanical without the express written permission of the author.

The views expressed in this work are solely those of the author and do not necessarily reflect the views of the publisher, and the publisher hereby disclaims any responsibility for them.

ISBN: 978-1-326-46892-7

PublishNation, London
www.publishnation.co.uk

INTRODUCTION

Switch on the television these days and there will almost certainly be a woman journalist reporting on the news whether on the home front, abroad in a war zone, or covering top sports events.

It was not always so. Only comparatively recently have women made their mark in what was once a man's world.

In the 1950s and 60s it was rare indeed. When I started work as a cub reporter on the local newspaper I was the only female in the office and one of only a few in the entire series of at least six newspapers covering north Kent.

We had all started work straight from school and it was a considerable time later that the first ever woman university graduate was to join us. The tide was turning in favour of women journalists.

The following is my story of what it was like to be among the first almost fifty years ago.

Chapter 1: THE INTERVIEW

The stage at the town hall must have been one of the most unusual settings ever for a job interview – self imposed at that.

My school, which had only 250 pupils and was not large enough to host concerts and prizegivings, held them in the town hall instead.

It was here in the 1950s, at one of these events, the awards were being presented by the Editor-in-Chief of the Kentish Times series of newspapers, John Massey.

I do not recall receiving any prize. At primary school I was given books for punctuality and diligence, not the sort of acclaim awarded to students these days, nor the sort they might want. Later, at the private school I attended, I did well at English and art but with the emphasis on mathematics I could not hope to receive any cherished book or certificate.

English was by far my favourite subject. I enjoyed writing essays, and, encouraged by my English master, Nicholas Seaton, a tall, swarthy, black haired man whose family came from Burma, I would write stories during the holidays which he would duly read and discuss with me on my return to school.

It was my dream, my ambition, to become a journalist, a newspaper reporter, and he spurred me on, encouraging me in every way.

One has to remember that at that time there were hardly any women journalists so it seemed a distant hope that I could ever become one, until that particular prize giving.

During the presentations and prolonged droning speeches I began to formulate a plan as I sat next to my mother in my crisp uniform of grey skirt, white blouse and red and black striped blazer. What if I could speak to the Editor of my aspirations? Perhaps he could advise me as to which course I should follow.

The idea increasingly took hold, until, as the final applause faded away and there was a general scraping of chairs and shuffling of papers as everyone prepared to leave, I took a deep breath and sidled up to the stage. My father was away on business but by my side suddenly appeared my friend's father. He must have guessed what I was up to and quietly took control of the situation.

He caught the eye of the Editor and smilingly introduced me. The Editor then beckoned me to join him and I ran up the steps to sit on one of the empty chairs on the stage beside him.

We then had a chat, in which he told me what exams I needed to pass before I could even consider entering journalism, and ended our impromptu little interview with the words: "Write to me when you have them".

I felt on cloud nine. The first step had been taken towards my goal and I was thrilled – until I was aware of several teachers hovering in the background clearly unimpressed by my hi-jacking their guest of honour and cornering him for an unplanned interview at such a time.

Mr. Seaton, 'Old Nick' as we called him behind his back, seemed to be filled with a mixture of both horror and admiration. "Cheek of the girl!" I heard him mutter under his breath.

It was worth the expected reprimands.

After much work I passed the necessary exams and applied to the newspaper for the job of trainee reporter. Initially I did not have much success simply because there had been a fire at the offices and they were not taking on any more staff.

I was advised to try again in a years' time. I spent those twelve months at commercial college learning shorthand and typing which I knew would come in useful whatever happened. I then wrote off again and this time landed the job, six months trial to see whether I liked the work - and more to the point whether the bosses were happy with me - and then, if mutually agreeable, three years apprenticeship.

It was one of the happiest days of my life.

Chapter 2: FIRST DAY

It was my first day and I was outside the Bexleyheath Observer office bright and early waiting for someone to arrive and unlock the door.

So that I did not seem too obviously the new girl I gazed intently through the bottle glass windows feigning interest in the black and white photographs on display of school sports days, fetes and presentations.

It was 9 a.m. on a Monday morning and no-one seemed in any hurry to get off to a quick start.

Eventually an elderly, stout lady came huffing and puffing along the road towards me.

"Hello, love" she beamed. "Not been waiting long, have you?"

"Oh, no" I lied.

She introduced herself as Mrs. Robinson – "Robbie to everyone here" – and after fiddling with a bunch of keys, opened the door and led the way inside.

Immediately in front of us was a long, highly polished wooden counter across which customers would place their advertisements. This was her domain.

At one side was a door leading to the back office, editorial, where there were four desks with a solid Imperial typewriter on each, and a spike.

On a table at one end of the room were huge files of backdated newspapers, the front page of each one almost identical in lay out to the last, with a photograph, top centre, of rows of men looking for all the world like some condensed school picture, except these were men of a certain age from organisations such as the Round Table, Rotary Club and Toc H.

Leading off from editorial was the editor's office, and either side of that the gents and ladies toilets which was the only one to boast a hand basin.

Until my arrival, Robbie had been the only woman there, and then more often in the front office than the back, so that the men reporters had developed a habit of racing straight from their toilet into the ladies to wash their hands without giving the matter a second thought.

I found I had to. With no lock on the door I soon learnt that to maintain any sort of privacy I had to jam one foot against the door to prevent any unwarranted intrusion while I was perhaps adjusting a stocking seam, or otherwise engaged.

At 17 years old and still adjusting to the world of work following school and college, where everyone was referred to as Sir or Madam, I found it hard to stop calling my colleagues, Mr. Mason and Mr. Jolly.

"Brian, please" and "I'm Peter" they would correct me.

The Editor, Ray Jones, was a quiet, calm man, who was a marvellous first boss, while Robbie, a motherly soul, would plod through the office with her kettle, ever ready to make a cup of tea.

As well as her duties in the front office and that of tea maker, she would sound the alert when the Editor arrived back late from a Rotary lunch, having seen his car enter the sideway leading to the car park at the back.

So from whatever we had been doing that we shouldn't have, by the time he walked through the door we presented a model picture of reporters hard at work, hammering out stories on our noisy machines.

Robbie was friend and confidante and would wade in where angels feared to tread if she felt anyone was being treated at all unjustly.

A former Salvationist, she would sit smoking in her sunny office overlooking the high street and the church opposite. Should she espy one of her anti-smoking Salvationist friends making their way to the office, more likely for a chat than to place an advertisement, as quick as a wink the cigarette would be whisked under the counter from where a tell-tale wisp of smoke would drift lazily upwards.

Although I never smoked, in those days, around 1960, reporters were positively encouraged to do so as a way of being sociable and to get people to open up and engage in conversation.

Drinking, too, was a rather different ballgame to now where most youngsters are familiar with every sort of drink going.

For me, and I was by no means alone in this, strange though it may sound now, the only drink I had up until starting work was a sherry at Christmas time.

Imagine how perplexed I was when I went to cover a flower show and was asked if I would like a gin and It (Italian Vermouth).

"Oh, yes please" I replied and swallowed the gin down in one go. What had the It got to do with anything, I wondered.

I soon found out as I struggled to take down columns of results against an every increasingly blurring background of red and yellow dahlias.

Before being let loose to get drunk at flower shows my first task was filing closely followed by writing up weddings and obituaries. Although considered small fry even these had their pitfalls and shortly before I started work the newspaper was taken to court for some discrepancy arising out of a wedding report.

I had to learn to conform with "the style of the house" as it was known, and the style permitted no such extravagances as "the happy couple" or "they left for a honeymoon at a secret destination".

As each wedding photograph came in the reporters would pour over them making comments such as "Poor mug, fancy marrying her" while the bride's dress was criticised with everyone adding their view as to how it could be improved. We fancied ourselves as experts.

I vowed there and then that should I ever get married a photograph and report would never appear in my local newspaper.

The flowing descriptions which arrived on my desk would include going-away outfits of lemon yellow or eggshell blue, or "she wore a stone outfit" – poor girl!

So it was that my first week passed by and in my scrapbook, marked in white pencil, August 8, 1960, I proudly stuck in my cuttings. A couple of wedding reports, an obituary, and a wage slip for £4 5s 6d.

Chapter 3: GETTING ABOUT

The roar of a motorbike thundering along the side of the office to the car park at the back signalled the return of one of the reporters.

There were three men on the staff and each had a bike. In 1960 this was how they got around.

At seventeen, and a raw cub reporter, my only way of getting to events was to walk, get a bus, or, on the very odd occasion travel in style in the Mayoral car when the Mayor was attending a function and his bored, but very helpful chauffeur, had nothing else to do.

I vividly recall Friday nights when I might have to attend a meeting in Welling and then have to walk back home past the Embassy Ballroom, the regular haunt of Teddy Boys with their greased back hair, velvet trimmed jackets, drainpipe trousers, bright fluorescent coloured socks and thick soled shoes.

Their presence was ominous and spelt trouble with bloody fights spilling out of the ballroom on to the street outside. I would press myself as close to the shop windows opposite as I could, slinking past in the hope that I would not be noticed.

As a result I was determined to get a car as soon as it was possible to do so – to be independent and safer.

I had to wait a long time as I was earning precious little to begin with but at nineteen I passed my driving test – albeit at the second attempt – and bought a grey, 1953 Ford Anglia. It cost me £135 and although I had been saving hard I was still in debt to my mother and father who had lent me a considerable sum towards it.

I called my car Rex, a mix of the registration letters, and he became a good friend as we travelled the highways and byways together. The bonnet had two flaps, each with grills open to the elements, but although for the most part the car was parked outside and not in a garage, it rarely failed to start first time.

If it did it could be crank started. It was also possible to double declutch, and, of course, there was no heating which meant driving around like a frozen iceberg in the middle of winter. The indicators were orange plastic arrows which would spring out at the flick of a switch unless hand signals were used which meant sticking the right arm out of the window and swivelling it around in a circular movement to indicate a left turn while tightly holding on to the steering wheel with the left hand.

What Rex did not like was to have more than two people on board. Two it could cope with. Four it could not. Not so bad on a straight flat road but when it came to a hill he refused point blank to go up unless the two people in the back got out. So out they would clamber while Rex chugged to the top and my front seat passenger and I sat there waiting for them to rejoin us, gasping for breath.

Because I lived in a house facing on to a busy road it was not always possible to cut across the flow of traffic and on to the driveway when arriving back home. Instead I would park up in a road beyond a swathe of grass and trees opposite until it was quiet enough to venture around and on to the drive.

On one particular occasion, unable to get Rex to start, my father obligingly came across and pushed it all the way round, quite some distance, while I steered.

It was only having negotiated the car on to the drive, and my father having collapsed with exhaustion on to the sofa, did I discover that the ignition had not been properly switched on! Well they say there is one born every minute.

Talking of which...One day I had just parked up near the office when a man who had been walking by suddenly stopped, smiled, leaned across the car and pressed his thumb on the windscreen.

My jaw dropped open. What was this weirdo up to? I opened the window and looked at him questioningly, upon which he withdrew his thumb and explained: "Well it does say press" pointing to my grand little PRESS sticker proudly displayed in one corner.

Rex was steady, reliable, but no speedster. On one occasion, unbelievably, I was pulled over for speeding by the police. It was impossible to go more than 40 miles an hour and I told the officer this. He let me off with a caution.

We went everywhere trundling along country lanes to grand old houses to interview someone or finding our way along rows of identical looking streets in south London.

On one occasion we turned into the drive of the plush local Conservative headquarters where Edward Heath MP, later to be Prime Minister, was being regally entertained by some admiring lady supporters, all with blue rinsed permed hair, the style adopted by many older ladies then.

My Editor-in-Chief was among the few men guests to have been invited and he waved a friendly acknowledgement in my direction as he drove up in his Humber, until, upon reversing into a parking spot I misjudged and landed in the flower bed instead, wheels spinning. Suddenly, and quite inexplicably, he realised he had made a mistake and that he didn't really know me after all.

Years later when I was reporting for the Kent Messenger every journalist was allotted a bright yellow Mini van until eventually the company progressed to owning a fleet of glossy Fiats.

This was driving with everything paid for. I would be busy typing some copy when a new tax disc would appear on my desk or a reminder to take the car in for servicing.

In the large company car park, which boasted its own petrol pump, regular vehicle checks would be carried out in strict military fashion. A long line of cars would face the office manager who had the bearing and vocal chords equal to that of an sergeant major as he bellowed instructions: "Right indicators – on! Left – on! Side lights – on! And full – and dipped!!

Every command was promptly obeyed in this synchronised display which must have been well worth watching.

Chapter 4: ALL TYPES

It takes all types to make a world and those with zest, go, and a spirit of adventure, are often found in a newspaper office.

In common with most adventurers they are usually roamers, too, resulting in a rapid turn over of staff much to the consternation of the editor.

Within the space of just two years in one office we had an assortment of different characters among them Francois, the South African, with fair, wavy hair, light blue blazer and immaculately pressed trousers.

He was forever embroiled in fierce, political arguments with Margaret, a spirited, Irish girl, who later went to live in New York.

There was Frank, a middle-aged, greying man, who would shuffle around in his suede shoes. Easy-going, good hearted and friendly he had an amazing knack of wheedling his way around people to get what he wanted.

Then there was Sheila, a vivacious, witty girl, who held great parties in her top floor flat much to everyone's delight but her neighbours.

At one there were rows and rows of cigarette vans lining the drive and the road outside, a giveaway that her latest boyfriend was a 'rep' for a cigarette company.

Another time we had a highly-strung, nervous girl on the reporting staff whose husband was based at another of the branch offices. She rarely spoke to any of us and spent ages making mysterious phone calls. We arrived one morning to find her gone.

So was her husband. All they left behind them was a trail of bad debts.

Chris was a trainee reporter, like myself, and into music in a big way. Tall and gangling he would sit on the window sill, feet on his chair, leaning intently over his desk where he would hammer away using two pencils as makeshift drumsticks.

It was not a big surprise that he went on to join one of the big musical journals.

Such a hotchpotch of characters and yet we all got on so well.

Every Wednesday afternoon, when the editor was away at the paper's head office as the paper was being put to bed, we would push back the desks and chairs, fish out an old ruler and a ping pong ball, and play our very own game of cricket with its distinctive rules.

Points were awarded for hitting the skirting board or ceiling or if the ball happened to fly out of the open window.

There were other crazy times when we took exaggerated photographs such as Chris portraying a really high powered reporter, pounding away on his typewriter surrounded by telephones, spikes, directories, file trays and mountains of paperwork.

Another was of a reporter falling out of a cupboard clasping a dagger to his heart. What the shoppers must have thought if they happened to glance into our office on their way to the car park just at that crucial point, goodness knows.

In yet another we attempted to capture something of the Dickensian image with one of the young trainees sitting on top of a high cupboard, his legs dangling down over the side with a huge and weighty bound newspaper file spread open across his lap.

Oh, those Wednesday afternoons. I don't remember us ever getting caught out thanks to the ever vigilant Robbie keeping her eyes open for the return of the editor's car from her vantage point in the front office.

There was just one rather big gaffe I made shortly after beginning work.

It was not unusual for members of the public to stroll in to see us about a story or hand in a report.

On this particular occasion a somewhat distinguished looking man wandered in, glanced around in a superior way, quietly perused the file of back dated copies, and then strode out again.

We had all been eyeing this performance in awed silence.

"Anyone would think he owned the place" I commented.

"He does!" chorused everyone together.

Chapter 5: SCOOP

I was going to a dance – or that had been the plan.

"See you outside Chiesman's, Lewisham, 7.30" said my friends. So, in good time, all dressed up in my finery and very high heeled shoes, I trotted off on the ten minute walk to the station.

It was a freezing cold, dark winter's evening and as I made my way along the quiet suburban streets the only sign of movement came from the flickering television screens in cosy front rooms where the curtains had not yet been pulled together.

On arriving at the station I bought my ticket and ventured out on to the platform. Only two other people were there, stamping their feet in a vain attempt at keeping warm.

A tinny sounding bell pierced the night air somewhere out of sight along the line followed by a signal jolting and clanging into place.

No other sound. Just a general feeling of expectancy as we stared into the darkness willing our train to appear while the elderly porter consulted his watch and glanced agitatedly up at the large station clock.

The platform opposite was empty. No-one to even watch. Just a row of advertising placards proclaiming the merits of everything from soup to religion.

Then something of interest to focus upon. A Royal Mail van trundled down the opposite approach and reversed up to where two gates were open leading on to the platform.

I idly watched as the driver jumped out, humped a bulging mailbag from out of the back and slinging it across one shoulder made his way to the platform, presumably to load on to the next train.

Suddenly three figures loomed out of the darkness, attacked the startled postman and grabbed his bag.

As one repeatedly rained blows with what appeared to be a cosh, the others ran up the slope to the railway bridge where a car was waiting, engine running. The attacker finally left the postman in a crumpled heap on the ground and ran to join his accomplices in the car which screeched off into the night.

The dazed postman struggled to his feet, leant into the van and set off an alarm which blared deafeningly.

It had all happened so fast that a few more seconds elapsed before the little audience, who had been watching in utter disbelief, were shaken into action.

The station, which had been so deathly quiet only moments before, burst into a frenzy of furious activity. From being hardly anyone around there seemed to be people everywhere running and shouting.

What to do first in my role as newspaper reporter? Interview witnesses, the stationmaster, ring the national newspapers and my editor, who had, with good reason, earned the nickname, 'the lineage king'.

Somehow things sorted themselves out and after gathering a few facts and quotes together I tore out of the station and into the nearest telephone kiosk. It was out of order. Maybe the work of the gang. Who knows, but I ran up the approach to the next box where that phone, too, was out of order.

It was 1961, long before the advent of mobile phones, and with not another public phone anywhere around and no taxi in sight, there was nothing for it but to run the short distance home, which had never seemed so far away.

I was dressed for a dance, not for running a two minute mile, and there I was going as hard as I could, desperately trying to avoid getting my stiletto heels caught in the pavement cracks.

At last I was home, hurtling through the front door and making straight for the phone.

The telephone bill for that evening's calls was exorbitant, but then so was my lineage.

I got £10, a lot of money then, with the added distinction of such bylines as Sunday Telegraph Reporter, Reynolds News Reporter and many others besides.

Having seen it all with my own eyes I was able to provide a graphic and colourful first hand account.

The robbers got away with £1,000 which was to have been loaded on to the London bound train and was one of several such raids to be carried out in the south of England at that time.

They were never caught. The exercise had been scrupulously organised down to the very last detail.

What turned out to be a stolen grey Austin van had been parked against the wall preventing the mail van driver from parking in his usual place but forcing him instead to back down to the gate. This left him only the width of the pavement to cross with his mailbag making him an easy target.

While one man acted as look-out on the railway bridge the other three waited, hidden under cover of darkness, for the tip-off that the van had left the sorting office and was on its way.

By the time the Observer came out the following Thursday the story was stale news and had to be re-angled on the lines of the search.

Never mind. Within my first year I had got a scoop!

Chapter 6: THE RAW SIDE

Back in those early days it was the reporters lot to get the names of all the babies born on Christmas Day and New Year's Day and write captions to go with the photographs of beaming mothers cuddling their offspring. I was always afraid that in my festive, befuddled state, I would get the names wrong and attribute a parent with the wrong child.

At least that was light and pleasant. What was not so agreeable were the too frequent brushes with death, whether it be to interview the family of a car crash victim or even the relatives of someone who had been murdered. This was virtually unknown in my early days as a reporter when the file contained only one murder having occurred in years and years. Sadly as time went on this was to gradually pad out as it became more of a regular occurrence.

In a corner of the office was also a filing cabinet referred to as 'The Graveyard' containing pre-written obituaries ready to pull out and publish just as soon as someone of local prominence died.

A weekly task for the junior reporter was to check out whether this had happened by visiting the undertakers.

It always impressed me when I called in at the pokey little office, for there, as it were ready and waiting, would be a black top hat and a pair of suede gloves perched on the table by the door as if just waiting to be snatched up and pressed into service.

Without waiting for me to even ask the receptionist would look up and say, matter of factly, "No, dear, we haven't got any for you this week".

While this appeared rather flippant, I was soon made aware of just how harrowing it can be to lose someone in tragic circumstances when my fiancé was killed in a car crash.

From then on I particularly dreaded being assigned the task of interviewing a recently bereaved family. It is the most unenviable job having to call on someone in these circumstances although I invariably found they seemed to welcome the opportunity to speak to a stranger and often I was asked to call again.

Everyone has their own way of dealing with tragedy, either accepting or refusing to face up to what has happened. Many a time relatives rang the newspaper office the same morning their dear one had died to tell us about it and ask for a report to be published.

When someone of prominence such as a past Mayor died this would usually result in a big funeral in Christ Church just across the road.

Shortly beforehand it was a reporter's task to place little white cards on all the pews for mourners to complete with their name and status.

The alternative to them not being put out in this way was for the unfortunate reporter to stand at the church door, like a little vulture, handing them to people as they filed in.

Following the service came the job of collecting them all up again, returning to the office and writing up the report compiling the interminable list of mourners in strict order of seniority.

Every aspect of death is experienced sooner or later.

I well remember a bitterly cold, snowy, February day – my 20th birthday – when I had to drive out to a caravan site in the wilds of the countryside late afternoon to investigate the deaths of two elderly spinster sisters.

The whole area was crawling with police and the caravan in which the women had been found was drab and dirty with torn curtains hanging raggedly at the windows.

A policeman told me not to go too near and I was only too pleased to do as he said as the place reeked even from where I was standing some distance away.

I spent some time trying to build up a picture of the two women and their lives by interviewing people living in neighbouring caravans and the owner of the local grocer's shop, but, amazingly, no-one seemed to know anything about them.

It seemed they were recluses who died from self-neglect with no-one at all aware of their plight.

On another occasion, this time by contrast a scorching hot summer's day, I had to go to a building site where a trench had caved in on top of a labourer.

The man's workmates, stripped to the waist, were frantically shovelling away earth in a desperate attempt to rescue him.

Ambulances and fire engines, sirens blaring, screeched up to the trench, but too late to be of any use. The men, exhausted and riven with sweat, found to their horror that instead of digging earth away from their trapped colleague, they had been piling it on top of him instead.

Never before have I seen strong, tough men on the brink of breaking down as they realised what they had done, and it is something I hope never to see again.

As for actually seeing a dead person, the first I ever saw was a Romany gipsy lying in state surrounded by banks of flowers.

He was held in high esteem by the travelling community and the newspaper had been invited to send someone to the pre-funeral gathering. It fell to me to go and I drove out to a pub called The Startled Saint in the middle of the countryside. Convoys of caravans, trucks and battered old cars were streaming into an adjoining field.

It seemed that every Romany from every corner of Britain was descending on this small corner of Kent to pay their last respects. The old and the young, women with babies in their arms, all milling quietly around. Everyone eyed me suspiciously as I stood for a moment wondering where to go. Then a swarthy man with iron grey hair appeared at my side.

"You from the paper?" he asked, and when I nodded he grabbed my elbow and propelled me towards a large tent, pulled back the flap and ushered me roughly inside.

My first impression was of a number of men standing silently and protectively around the corpse. I was the only woman present and acutely aware of scores of dark brown eyes boring into me closely watching my reaction.

I briefly looked at the face of the dead man, retaining an image of a sallow face and closed eyes, and cast my own eyes downwards in what I hoped might be interpreted as a respectful gesture. I remained like that for what seemed an eternity, although it could have only been a few minutes, before my guide touched me on the shoulder as a signal that it was time to leave.

This dramatic close-up of a traditional ritual was to be forever etched in my memory.

In fact trying to do the right thing is not always easy.

One Christmas a man came into the office asking if we could carry a story appealing to his missing wife to come home. He told how he and his children were heartbroken after she left never to return. Whatever was worrying her could be sorted out, he said, and if she would only come back it would be their best Christmas present ever.

A photograph of him and his children sitting by their Christmas tree appeared in the paper accompanied by a touching little story.

The result was that his wife saw the picture and story and returned home. Any satisfaction I may have felt at have helped to reunite this little family turned out to be fleeting. In fact guilt may have been a better description when only two weeks later the wife was murdered by her husband, stabbed to death in the kitchen of their home.

Another job was to cover inquests, sometime two or three during the course of one morning alone.

These could range from accidents to suicides and without exception seemed to be conducted in gloomy, ill-lit rooms where the family of the deceased would sit on rows of hard wooden chairs, hunched forwards straining to catch the softly spoken words of the coroner or pathologist.

It must have been some compulsive urge to boost his psyche in such a morbid profession but one of the pathologists regularly displayed the only dash of colour in these drab, grey surroundings, when he crossed his legs to reveal dazzling bright red socks.

All eyes would be drawn, as if magnetised, to what appeared to be an almost irreverent fashion statement. It was as if he was saying "All right, Death, you might be master today but I am going to cock a snook at you while I can. My socks for starters!"

Then, when the time came for him to read his report, he would stand up, the hems of his trousers would drop down a fraction to respectfully cover the frivolous socks, and he would reel off an incomprehensible list of internal medical disorders. These would be accompanied by equally baffling explanations which only members of the medical profession were likely to understand.

This would do nothing to satisfy the urgent need of the relatives to discover exactly what had happened to their nearest and dearest and who were usually left looking puzzled and perplexed as, his report concluded, he made his apologies to the coroner and hastily left the room.

Meanwhile, at lunchtime a group of us used to regularly frequent a small restaurant near the office where among the clientele was a tall, gaunt faced undertaker, usually still attired in his black funeral clothes.

As we trooped in he would eye one of us up and down as if mentally measuring for an imminent departure, and, with a twinkle in his eye, would remark "Oh dear, you are not looking at all well today!"

Chapter 7: THE SILLY SEASON

"Come on or we will be late!"

We tumbled into Rex, my old banger, and shot off down the road at full speed, waving to a car load of compositors – comps as they were known – also returning to the newspaper office after a lunch hour spent at the nearby open swimming pool.

Wet, straggly hair clung to our foreheads as we arrived back to hang our colourful costumes and towels out of the window to dry, in full view of the high street.

At this time of year, August, when the schools had broken up for the long summer holidays, and most people were away, everything seemed to stop. There were few diary jobs to cover and a general shortage of news with which to fill the paper each week.

"We will never do it" wailed the Editor. "Work up a few specials".

It was then that weird stories that would never normally be published were gratefully snatched at to fill the empty pages. Stories of ghosts in the nearby caves and pictures of tall sunflowers.

So, with the Silly Season as it was known, in full swing, we made the most of those lazy, hazy summer days. Lunchtimes filled with tennis in the park, swimming at the pool or picnicking on the Common.

On one occasion I heard that a lorry driver in the area had won a big money prize on a television programme. Details were not given out then and hard as I tried I just could not track him down.

By sheer luck, as it happened, I and another girl reporter were tucking into our sandwich lunch on the Common, the day before Press day, when up purred a Noddy bike, as the little police bikes were called, with one of the village's jolly policeman sitting astride it.

"Hello" he called out, "and how are we today?"

I don't know that he was ever supposed to but when he heard the story of my futile search, he looked around as though expecting the Chief of Police to step out from behind a bush, and whispered where I might find the lucky winner.

My day was made. Several times I called at the house to find no-one in but perseverance paid off and eventually I got my story.

Sometimes getting to the root of a story could be misconstrued as criminal intent. Once I called on a superb house in a private road in a select area. After knocking and ringing for some time I decided I would have to return later and walked back to my car.

I was just preparing to drive off when in my rear mirror I caught sight of a policeman striding purposefully towards me. When he recognised me he looked almost disappointed as apparently he had been under the impression that I was 'casing the joint' in preparation for breaking and entering.

Another amusing incident was my search for a large white slab of stone rumoured to have mysteriously appeared on the Common, which was being considered locally as having links to witchcraft and black magic rituals.

I trekked along paths and through bracken in my search but found nothing. It was then I came across a lady sitting on a seat enjoying the morning sunshine and I asked her if she had seen anything resembling the white stone.

No, she said, she hadn't heard about it and could she help me find it. She went one way and I the other while her dog took the middle route. We met back at the seat still with nothing to report.

I thanked her and left while she, still intrigued by the story, continued to thrash her way through the undergrowth, her dog close at heel.

My next attempt to solve the growing mystery was to call on one of the local Commons Conservators who owned a nearby bookshop.

When he heard my tale he at first looked puzzled and then laughed.

The slab of stone, he told me, when he had at last gathered his composure, was no more than the base for a new seat, the seat my lady had been sitting on when I approached her.

Another crazy story bore the somewhat exaggerated headline 'Midnight Cattle Stampede'. Well, it sounded something even though it had involved only four cows ambling through an open gate on to the road.

The story had got out of all proportion by a bus driver returning his vehicle to the depot late at night. Suddenly confronted by cows coming towards him he later said he felt like Cheyenne.

Conductors and drivers herded the cows into the car park of a local factory though next morning they had mysteriously disappeared, apparently back to their farm.

The police who we contacted next morning claimed to know nothing of the incident.

"We got our milk as usual this morning" one said.

Proof that it had not been all a dream came when the factory workers turned up to be greeted by the waft of manure drifting through the car park.

In Silly Season time it was no surprise to receive strange telephone calls such as the one from someone claiming to have hoopoo birds on his lawn while yet another was triumphant that he had a yucca tree in bloom.

Apparently yuccas only bloom once in every seven years but immediately after a photograph of one had appeared not to be outdone a whole spate of others cropped up.

Still on the humorous aspects of reporting funny stories and incidents, many would occur which could not always be published. There was the time the Mayor dropped his jelly on the carpeted floor of the newly opened old peoples' home or when the Bishop nearly lost his mitre as he passed beneath a perilously low arch.

Another last ditch, desperate way of filling up those Silly Season blank pages was by writing a feature on your last holiday though even this could wear rather thin after a while.

"Oh no, not again" was a so called friend's response to another article I had written along these lines.

Still on the silly theme, but at a different time of year, was April Fools Day, when many a trick was played much to the readers delight.

One tale involved large ships ostensibly sailing up the River Medway to dock at Maidstone, an impossible feat bearing in mind the shallow depth of water there not to mention the many locks along the way which would have to have been miraculously negotiated.

And what about the famous story concerning the Tovil treacle mines.

Tovil is an area of Maidstone with its claim to fame little more than a built up area of houses which mysteriously found itself on the map for its productive treacle mines.

So where were they everyone was asking, until they noticed the date above the article, April 1.

Many years later the mere mention of them brought a smile to the reporters faces in the newsroom. "Oh, yes" they would say, "how could anyone forget the Tovil treacle mines!"

Chapter 8: GOING TO THE DOGS

Quite frankly at 23 I considered myself past the age of such childish complaints as tonsillitis, but here I was on my very birthday feeling sick and disillusioned that life could play such a rotten trick.

All week I had felt under the weather with everything a bit of an effort and when the news editor stopped me in the corridor to ask whether I liked dogs I knew I had to tread carefully or land myself with a lot of work which I really didn't feel up to.

I knew from past experience that, roughly translated, his question really equated to "Crufts Dog Show is on this week and I want you to go and sort out the local results".

The very thought of traipsing round a dog show with my throat stinging, eyes watering and legs shaking sent me into a mental whirl. So in answer to his question I warily replied: "They are all right".

"You either do or you don't" he retorted, his pipe chattering against his teeth. "Do you?"

My resolve to stand fast evaporated. "Yes" I weakly replied.

Without another word he made for his office. 'Oh, no, you don't' I thought to myself. The idea of being held in suspense until possibly Friday evening as to my fate was too much to contemplate.

I followed him in: "If you are thinking of sending me to the dog show, Sir, I would rather not go this Saturday. You see I am feeling pretty lousy." Honesty, I thought, was the best policy.

His look, which I half expected to confirm with a raised eyebrow that I was lousy, surprisingly softened. Then he said: "Oh it's not this Saturday but the next!"

Worse still, that was supposed to be my Saturday off.

I needn't have worried. That same weekend I was feeling so ill I had no option but to go to the doctor's surgery, where, ironically, the only other patient was a little boy suffering from a dog bite.

He disappeared into the doctor's room and seconds later there was a piercing yell. He emerged clutching his arm and crying while his mother tried to comfort him.

It was my turn next. The doctor was young, pleasant, and frighteningly efficient. He rebuked me for not having gone to see him earlier and announced that as the shops were shut he would have to give me a penicillin injection to tide me over, and where would I like it, in the leg or bottom?

I was on the verge of suggesting the leg when he beat me to it.

"I think the bottom would be the best place". Horrors.

A few minutes later I was limping out of the surgery clutching a prescription in one hand and my bottom with the other.

I was off work for a time and when I did begin to feel a little better had my spirits somewhat dampened by a so-called get well message from the News Editor. My mother took the call in which he said: "Give her my best wishes and tell her ladyship that we are struggling on without her."

What made it worse was that I was sure that they were.

Chapter 9: OUT ON STRIKE

The bitter cold winter of 1978 saw the National Union of Journalists call out its members on strike.

Thousands marched in an all out war against what were described as 'miserably low wages' in the Newspaper Society sector.

About 8000 took part in the strike – the first of its kind in the Union's 71 year history.

According to a special issue of The Journalist, published on December 6, practically every weekly newspaper chapel in England and Wales had walked out at noon with all but a handful of daily chapels doing the same.

All were loyally responding to the Union Executive's call for an indefinite strike and where I worked at the Kent Messenger the majority came out after meetings in the crowded, smoke filled upper room, of a local pub.

It was difficult. We had no particular axe to grind as we were well paid and the conditions were good, but we were also only too well aware that in many newspaper offices juniors were overworked and grossly underpaid.

As members of the National Union of Journalists, which looked after everyone's interests, we were obliged to obey the call for strike action.

The consequences were dire. We were locked out of the offices and our company vehicles taken away from us.

All members of the NUJ employed by South Eastern Newspapers received a letter from the Editorial Director.

It read:

'The industrial action the National Union of Journalists has instructed its members to take may constitute, if followed, a breach of contract by the individuals concerned.

' I am therefor advising you, as an NUJ member, that if you impose any such sanctions or inhibitions on your own duties you are liable to be suspended from duty immediately without pay and will forfeit all allowances and flat-rate expenses until you agree to normal working'.

Every day, instead of driving to work, I would catch the train to the office's nearby Larkfield Railway Station, and join my fellow journalists on the picket line.

Only one or two had defied the Union and carried on working alongside the few members of the Institute of Journalists which was unaffected.

As the weeks dragged by with no apparent end to the dispute in sight it became harder and harder to remain resolute.

No money was coming in to pay mortgages and keep financially afloat, at least one marriage hit the rocks as a result of the tension and loss of earnings, and the bitterness and resentment between those obeying instructions out in the cold and those inside in the warm being paid was to take many years to overcome.

Eventually cracks began to appear in the once solid wall as some were left with no choice but to go against the official line and return to work.

After about six weeks I was one and in the course of time was fined by the Union.

The end of the national action saw the NUJ win a good pay rise for its members and a return to work for everyone. It had been a terribly hard time trying to do the right thing and with consciences and loyalties being pulled in all directions.

Relieved that it was over at last how we prayed we would never be placed in such a situation again.

Chapter 10: THE COURTS

The Crown Court was a huge, imposing building. The Court Reporting Agency for whom I worked for many years, had an office on the ground floor from where a small team of reporters would send copy to the national and local newspapers.

All eight courts would be permanently busy with cases ranging from theft and fraud to murder. Scurrying on their way, black gowns billowing behind them, would be the bewigged barristers, clutching piles of documents tied up with ribbon.

Because there were only a few reporters there was not the time for one person to sit through an entire trial hearing a blow by blow account. The main point was to cover the opening by the prosecution, outlining what it was all about, then get the defence, and if any relevant details were still missing tie up the loose ends when the Judge delivered his summing up prior to the jury retiring to consider its verdict.

It was fascinating watching and listening to the barristers as well as observing the body language of defendants and witnesses. Was this man guilty or not? Did this sweet looking woman really behave as badly as was alleged?

In fact our copy was littered with such safely guarded words as alleged, maintained, appeared and seemed, to name but a few. The threat of legal action against us was ever present and we had to keep abreast of current changes in the law to be acutely aware of exactly what we were, or were not, entitled to publish.

It was in the absorbing but heavily restrained surroundings of the court that a little light relief lifted the atmosphere from time to time, and it came in various forms.

In one case a defendant who had just been told he was to be jailed for drug smuggling leant across the rail of the dock and loudly swore at the Judge who completely ignored him and began studying his papers relating to the next case.

Anxious to avoid any further embarrassment, two burly prison officers appeared each side of the man, gripped his arms and led him away in the direction of the lift and cells below.

Moments later the silence of the courtroom was broken by the sound of a clanking aluminium bucket being kicked against a brick wall in anger.

In the court eyebrows were raised and eyes twinkled. No-one dare say a word. The Judge, as unperturbed as ever, looked up and peering over his bi-focals called out "Wheel on the next!"

Occasionally, when a case dragged on and became tediously repetitive, the probation officer sitting next to me would drop off to sleep, sometimes even softly snoring. I would try and distance myself from him as the sharp eyed Judge glared over in our direction while others in the courtroom began to titter with amusement.

The same probation officer once told me how he had been interviewing a defendant with a view to preparing a report when the boy became exasperated with the questioning, pushed his chair back and shouting at him to "F*** Off!" stormed out of the room.

"I was determined to go ahead with the report, warts and all" he said wryly, "so I wrote how he had told me, in effect, to go and make love elsewhere. I think those in authority were able to ascertain what was meant!"

By contrast with this bluntness, the charm and effusiveness of the barristers was always pleasing to behold. One, a lady with sharp intellect and a dry wit to match, was waiting outside a courtroom for her case to be called when she declared with perfect public school enunciation: "I am fed up with hanging around here like a bad smell".

One of the double doors leading into court was clearly marked "Use This Door" but despite this everyone kept using the other one which constantly slammed much to the mounting annoyance of the Judge.

At one stage a barrister awaiting a forthcoming case, walked in, and as usual the door slammed behind him. "Take a seat. Anywhere," called out the Judge testily. "Come along in."

It was not an ideal time to make a request but the barrister smiled disarmingly and politely asked if it was at all likely his case might come on before luncheon, although, of course, he added, he was not really very hopeful.

The Judge seemed to forget about banging doors. "Of course" he said. "I think we can manage that."

The barrister almost fell over his gown in his appreciation. "I am so very heartened" he gushed, "really heartened."

The Judges often made dry pronouncements. One was when a defendant charged with indecent exposure was told that as it was late morning his case would continue at 2p.m. Whether he realised what he was saying or not, and I suspect he did, we will never know, but there was stifled laughter as the Judge told the man in the dock: "Case is adjourned until after lunch. Hold yourself in readiness".

As for the tannoy announcements which came blaring into our office, many provided a source of amusement.

Once it sounded as if a shorn lamb was being asked to report to reception. In fact it was not the curly woolly variety but a young man named Sean Lamb whose parents must have had either a keen sense of humour or were completely unaware of how they had made their son the butt of so many jokes.

Another announcement regularly put out calls for a barrister by the name of Ernley Money although it sounded for all the world like "Earn the money" – very appropriate for the high earning professionals in the courts every day.

There were also funny incidents as the translators struggled to convey what was being said to the courts. A Vietnamese man who had been asked if on coming to this country there was anything the family still needed, replied that there was, a wood rope.

"A wood rope?" he was asked again, no-one understanding what he meant.

"YES, YES". The man was becoming impatient now and his voice became raised as he repeated his request. "A WOOD ROPE".

At long last all became clear. What he was wanting was a wardrobe.

Chapter 11: WRITE FOR MY SUPPER

As a reporter it was quite usual to be invited to the annual dinners of local clubs and organisations where, in return for being given a meal, you were expected to write a report.

I cannot count the number of dinners I have had at one function or another which I was able to enjoy until the Royal Toast when chairs were scraped back, everyone shuffled to their feet, and glasses were raised as everyone chorused "The Queen! God bless her!"

It was then a case of placing coffee to one side and producing notebook and pen in readiness for action.

Good stories could on occasion be reaped from them unless the speakers got carried away telling a stream of jokes no self-respecting newspaper would dream of publishing.

"Give us a good spread, won't you" would quip the jolly man sitting next to me who had just bought me a drink.

"I'll do my best" I would reply brightly, if not inwardly over optimistic.

"We will look forward to reading it in the paper next week" interjects someone else. My heart sinks.

Somehow, though, I survived, hoping as always they would have forgotten about the few brief paragraphs tucked away on an inside page by the time I popped up again the next year.

"Is your photographer coming?" would be another regular question, as though he was my personal responsibility, tucked under the bed at home.

Had to tread warily here.

"Well he should be coming, but we only have six covering the whole area and three are ill, and you know how it is when you get held up at a job........."

In a flash the look changes from sweetness and charm to a cold, accusing, steely stare.

"You promised".

"Yes, but......."

The heat is suddenly taken out of the situation by the arrival of the photographer. Madam Chairman then tells him what pictures she wants him to take while he quietly proceeds to do things his way.

The first dinner I covered was a never to be forgotten event. So unworldly was I that I didn't leave enough to drink in my glass when it came to the toasts, didn't know whether I should be sitting or standing at various times during the evening, and had to hazard a guess when asked whether I wanted black or white coffee.

Somehow I managed to produce an acceptable report apart from having to ring up the organisers to find out the names of who had presented the bouquets, and to whom. Yes, that sort of detail was needed then.

Little problems cropped up everywhere in those early days.

There was the special church service where I sat in the middle of the congregation observing the editorial rule not to take part as I was there merely to report.

The withering glances I received from the people towering around me flourishing their hymn books meaningfully in my direction, was nobody's business.

I weakly tried to retaliate by make a show of my notebook while taking down the address delivered from the pulpit, but knew it was a lost cause as far as those around me were concerned.

From then on I vowed that I would always sit at the back of the church, or, if I had to sit at the front, to take part in the service.

The two most common greetings flung at me time and again were: "What an interesting job you must have" or "I have never met a reporter before" looking at me as if I was some sort of curiosity.

People have varying opinions of journalists, some holding them in high esteem, other denigrating.

"Tell me what you have to do to enter the profession?" I would be asked and I would give a detailed account of the examinations needed to pass to be accepted and information on the course run by the National Union of Journalists.

It all sounds rather grand but no reporter should get too proud for the next moment they are just as likely to be squashed by a remark such as: "Anyone can write the tripe you turn out!"

Others tried to use their position in society to dictate what appeared, or their alleged links with the Editor-in-Chief of the series of newspapers.

"Oh, yes, old John's a great friend of mine" would say a distinguished looking man, leaning back in his chair and waving a fat cigar around in the air. Turning to his wife he would continue, "Do you remember, dear, the time we all went to......." and out would trot some tale of something they were all supposed to have done together.

On one occasion I took the liberty of passing on the regards of some 'friends' to 'John', the Editor. He looked at me blankly. "Never heard of them" he said, and continued on his way down the corridor to that little room to which only the most senior members of the firm held a key – the most private and upper class loo in the building.

Again, many people seemed to think the paper was fully operational seven days and nights a week with a reporter on standby ready to race to cover their event at a moments notice.

"I'm sorry, madam" our chief reporter would say, most politely, "but you must have known some time ago that you were holding this function. Why didn't you let us know sooner?"

To cover as many as three evening jobs a week was normal varying from a cocktail party to a long, drawn out council meeting where the members seemed to derive sadistic pleasure in prolonging 'any other business' at the end.

Just as I was feeling tired and jaded after working several evenings on the trot, as well as long and busy days, and vaguely wondering about the attractions of a steady nine to five job, the Editor would say something along the lines of: "I have some free tickets for a show here. Would you like them?" or "Will you pop up to The Savoy next week and cover the Miss Secretary Contest? We have a local girl taking part", or even more memorable when I went to the premier of The Young Ones and met a very youthful Cliff Richard.

Somehow everything in the garden was lovely again and all the old enthusiasm would come rushing back.

There was, after all, nothing to beat the sound of the printers hammering away on the stone, the clattering linotype machines and the thunderous roar of the giant presses churning out the next day's papers.

Rows of proof readers, sitting in pairs, ensured there were no mistakes, and as juniors our duties on Press Day included 'passing the pages' making doubly sure everything was in order.

There was terrific satisfaction to be had in opening the newspaper next day to see everything well laid out and presented, not to mention the tinge of pride and vanity at seeing a story bearing my by-line.

Great days!

14973250R00028

Printed in Great Britain
by Amazon.co.uk, Ltd.,
Marston Gate.